Retro Christmas
Cross Stitch

As appealing today as ever, the whimsical graphic style and color palette of the Atomic Era is a fun look for celebrating Christmas. Lee Fisher's cross stitch designs lend themselves to a variety of decorative projects.

Let Heaven & Nature Sing

LEISURE ARTS, INC. • Maumelle, Arkansas

4

8

10

12

14

22

29

18

26

Home Sweet Home

Home Sweet Home (117w x 136h)
14 count 8³/₈" x 9³/₄"
16 count 7³/₈" x 8¹/₂"
18 count 6¹/₂" x 7⁵/₈"

X	DMC	B'ST	COLOR
☆	blanc		white
◆	210		lavender
#	301		brown
	310	◿	black
$	400		dk brown
S	445		yellow
♥	666		red
m	702		green
✳	704		lt green
◇	913		jade
▲	3689		mauve
⫶	3766		blue
▨			Green areas indicate last rows of previous sections of design.

Home Sweet Home was stitched over two fabric threads on a 14¹/₂" x 16" piece of 28 count Lt. Mocha Cashel® linen *(approx. design size: 8³/₈" x 9³/₄")* using two strands of embroidery floss for Cross Stitches and one strand of floss for Backstitches. The design was framed in an 11" x 14" frame.

To Aubrey
From Santa

Home Sweet Home

X	DMC	B'ST	COLOR
☆	blanc		white
◆	210		lavender
#	301		brown
	310	◿	black
$	400		dk brown
S	445		yellow
♥	666		red
m	702		green
✳	704		lt green
◇	913		jade
▲	3689		mauve
✕	3766		blue

Green areas indicate last rows of previous sections of design.

Let Heaven & Nature Sing

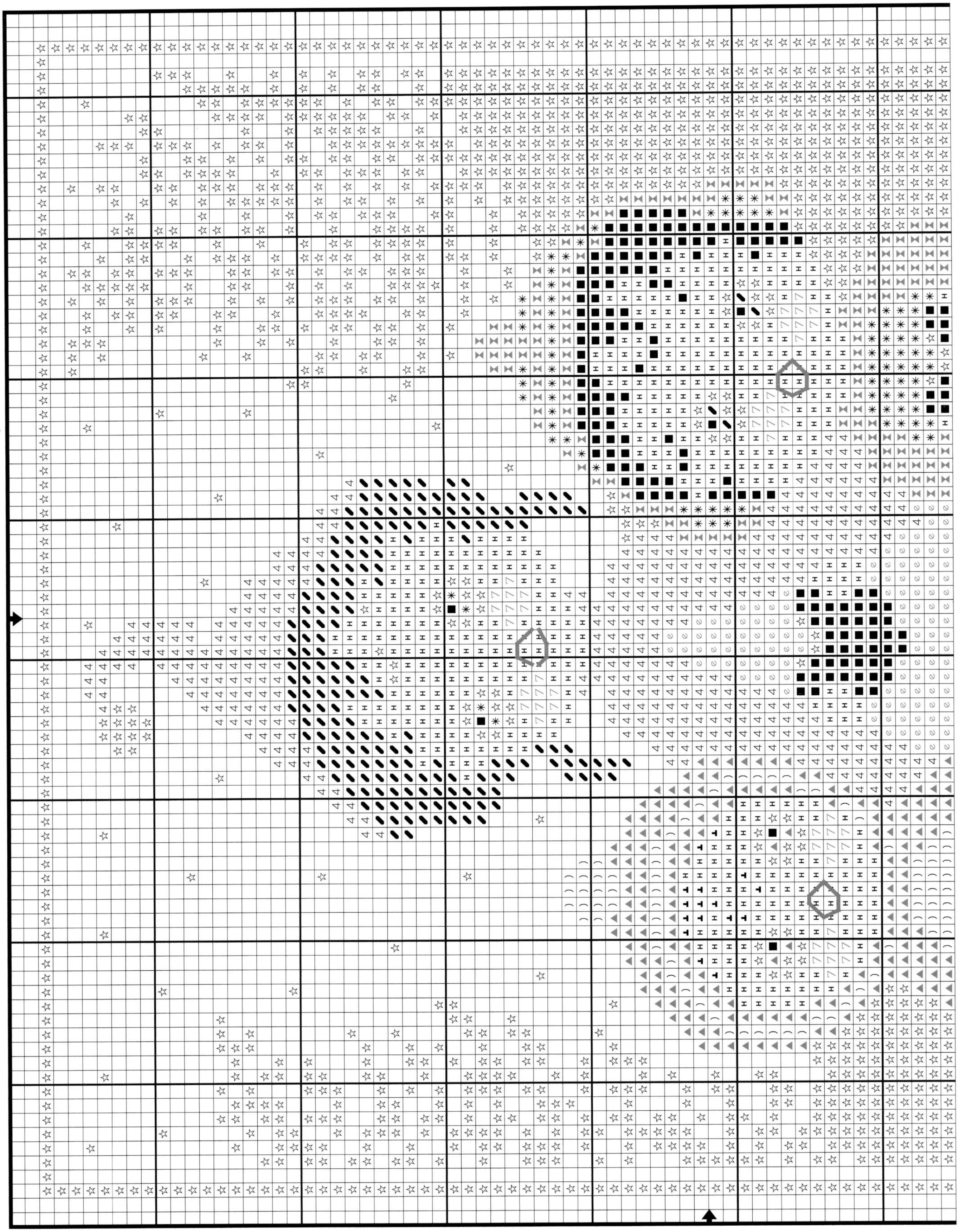

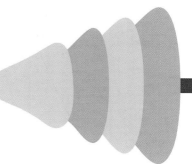

Let Heaven & Nature Sing
(82w x 92h)

14 count 5⁷/₈" x 6⁵/₈"
16 count 5¹/₈" x 5³/₄"
18 count 4⁵/₈" x 5¹/₈"

Let Heaven & Nature Sing was stitched over two fabric threads on a 12" x 13" piece of 28 count Glass Blue Lugana (*approx. design size: 5⁷/₈" x 6⁵/₈"*) using two strands of embroidery floss for Cross Stitches and one strand of floss for Backstitches unless otherwise noted. The design was matted and placed in a 12" x 12" frame.

X	DMC	B'ST	COLOR
H	948		lt peach
★	957		coral
⊠	967		peach
■	3371		vy dk brown
▶	3801		lt red
4	3805		magenta
)	3846		bright blue
▨			Green areas indicate last rows of previous sections of design.

♥ Use 2 strands of floss

X	DMC	B'ST	COLOR
☆	blanc		white
◆	151		lt pink
✳	164		lt green
◣	434		brown
⊘	552		purple
⋈	702		green
⊣	744		yellow
◀	807		turquoise
‡	817		red

9

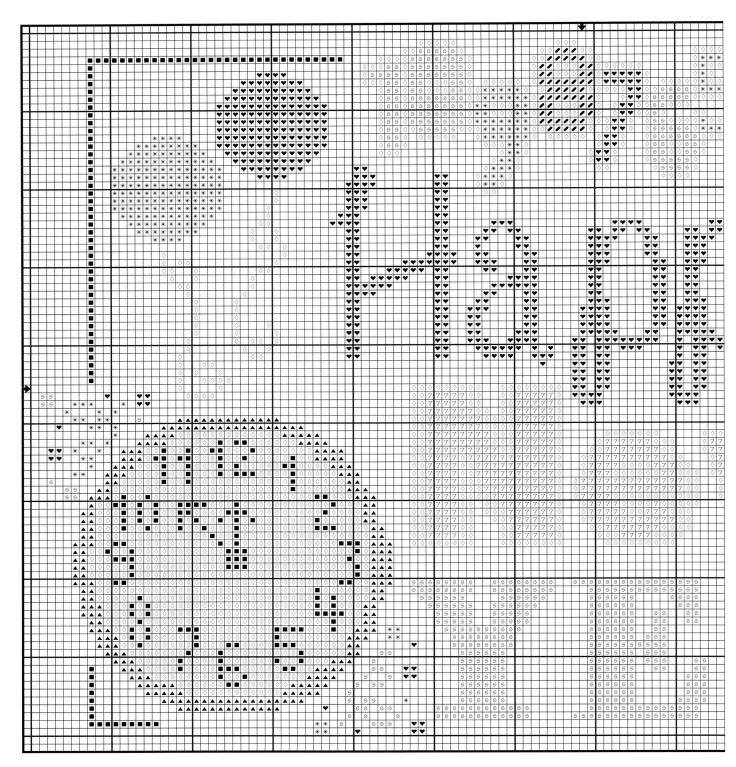

X	DMC	COLOR		X	DMC	COLOR
▲	157	blue		⑤	958	green
◇	318	grey (2 skeins		■	3799	dk grey
♥	349	lt red		✳	3853	orange
◢	472	yellow green		▨		Green areas indicate last rows
7	744	yellow				of previous sections of design.

Happy New Year (135w x 89h)
14 count 9$\frac{3}{4}$" x 6$\frac{3}{8}$"
16 count 8$\frac{1}{2}$" x 5$\frac{5}{8}$"
18 count 7$\frac{1}{2}$" x 5"

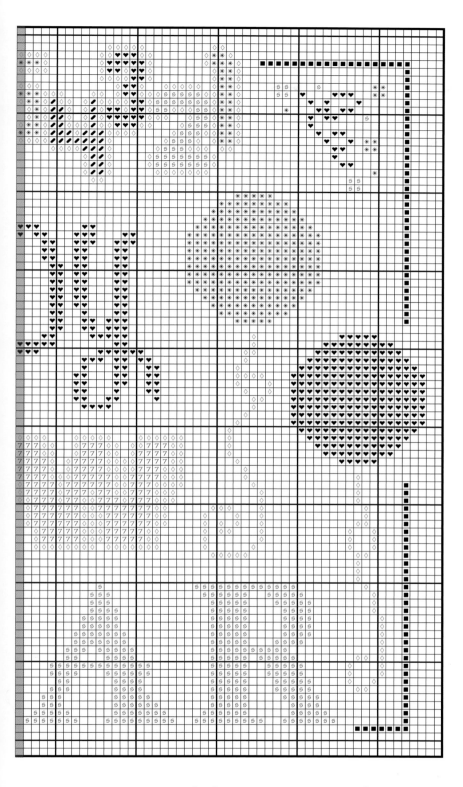

Happy New Year

PILLOW

You'll need fabric, lightweight fusible interfacing, and polyester fiberfill.

When sewing, always match the right sides and raw edges and use a 1/2" seam allowance.

1. Trim the stitched piece to the desired finished size plus 1/2" on all sides. Follow the manufacturer's instructions to fuse interfacing to the wrong side of the stitched piece.

2. Cut two fabric strips 3 1/2" wide and the same height as the stitched piece. Sew the strips to the side edges of the stitched piece. Press the seam allowances open.

3. Cut two fabric strips 3 1/2" wide and the same width as the stitched piece with the attached fabric strips. Sew the strips to the top and bottom of the stitched piece and strips. Press the seam allowances open.

4. Cut the pillow back the same size as the pillow front. Sew the pillow front to the pillow back, leaving an opening for turning. Clip the corners, turn right side out, and press. Stuff with fiberfill. Slipstitch the opening closed.

Happy New Year was stitched on a 16" x 12 1/2" piece of 14 count Stardust® Gold Dusted Aida (*approx. design size: 9 3/4" x 6 3/8"*) using two strands of embroidery floss for Cross Stitches. The design was made into a pillow.

My Deer Friend (59w x 117h)

14 count 4¼" x 8⅜"
16 count 3¾" x 7⅜"
18 count 3⅜" x 6½"

X	DMC	B'ST	COLOR
☆	blanc		white
+	300		dk brown
⌄	435	◹	brown
⊗	453		grey
⌐	603	◹	pink
⊞	606		red orange
⋈	676		gold
H	3348		yellow green
⊗	3607		magenta
◆	3766		blue
⌐	3814		teal
5	3846		turquoise
▦			Green area indicates last row of previous section of design.

My Deer Friend was stitched on a 10½" x 14½" piece of 14 count Ivory Aida (*approx. design size: 4¼" x 8⅜"*) using two strands of embroidery floss for Cross Stitches and one strand of floss for Backstitches. The design was made into a wine bottle bag.

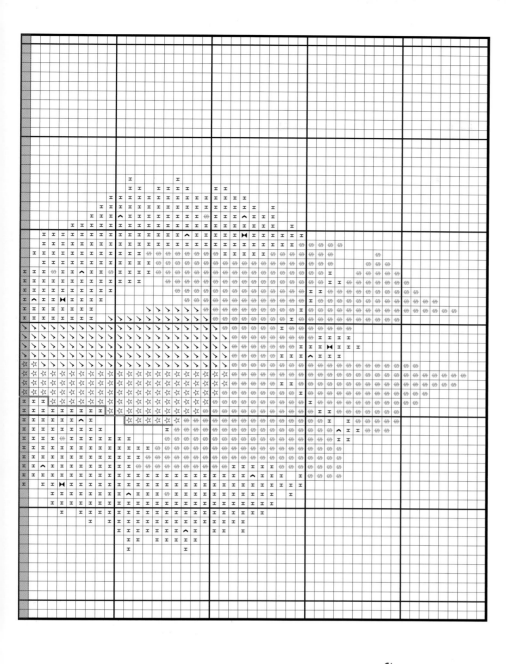

WINE BOTTLE BAG

You'll need fabric, coordinating embroidery floss, 22" length of gold cord, lightweight fusible interfacing, and paper-backed fusible web.

When sewing, always match the right sides and raw edges and use a ½" seam allowance.

1. Work Running Stitches (over and under 2 squares) around the stitched design, leaving 2 squares between the design and the Running Stitches. Trim the stitched piece ³⁄₈" from the Running Stitches. Fray the edges by removing fabric threads until you are 2 squares from the Running Stitches. Follow the manufacturer's instructions to fuse paper-backed fusible web to the wrong side of the stitched piece (do not apply web to the frayed areas).

2. Cut a 13" x 23½" fabric piece. Follow the manufacturer's instructions to fuse the interfacing to the wrong side of the fabric. Matching the long sides, fold the fabric in half and sew together along the bottom and side edges. Press the seam allowances open.

3. To create the boxed bottom, refer to **Fig. 1** to match the bottom seam to the side seam and opposite side; sew across each point. Trim the excess fabric. Turn the bag to the right side and press.

4. Remove the paper backing from the stitched piece. Flatten the bag. Center and fuse the stitched piece about 1" from the bag bottom. Press ½" to the wrong side on the bag opening; press 5½" to the wrong side again. Tie a knot at each cord end. Place a wine bottle in the bag and tie closed with cord.

Fig. 1

1³⁄₈"

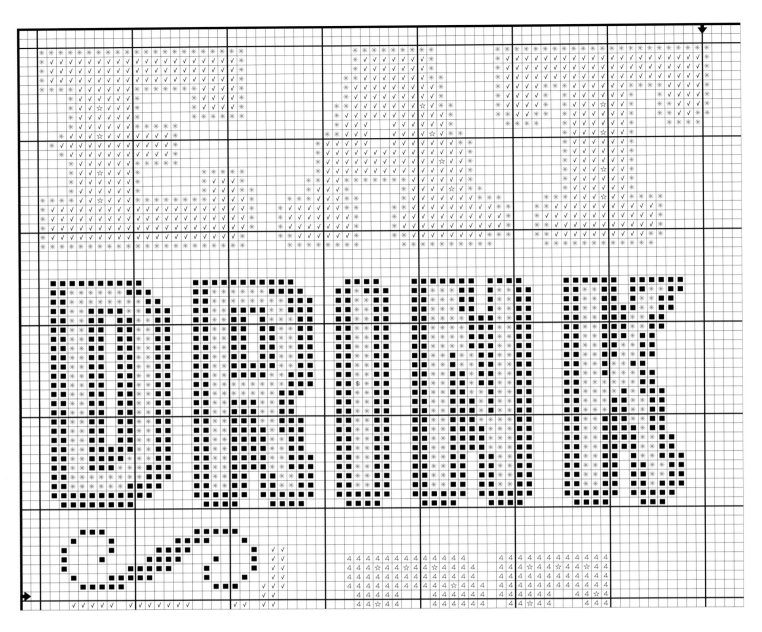

Eat Drink & Be Merry

X	DMC	COLOR
☆	blanc	white
⋒	209	lavender
♥	321	red
▰	407	sand
4	727	yellow
$	913	green

X	DMC	COLOR
7	948	peach
√	3340	apricot
◆	3689	mauve
✳	3766	teal
■	3799	vy dk grey
▨	Green areas indicate last rows of previous sections of design.	

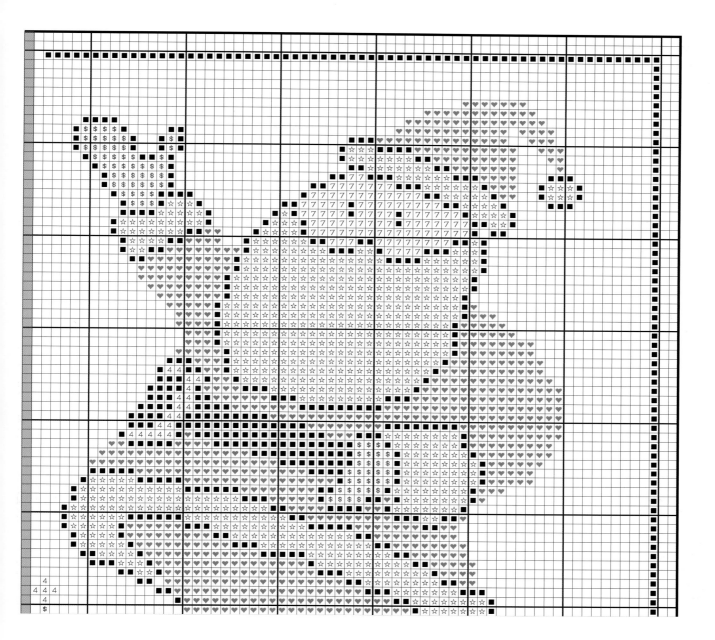

Eat Drink & Be Merry was stitched on a 16" x 14¹/₂" piece of 14 count White Aida *(approx. design size: 10" x 8¹/₂")* using two strands of embroidery floss for Cross Stitches. The design was framed in an 11" x 14" frame.

Eat, Drink & Be Merry (140w x 119h)
14 count 10" x 8¹/₂"
16 count 8³/₄" x 7¹/₂"
18 count 7⁷/₈" x 6⁵/₈"

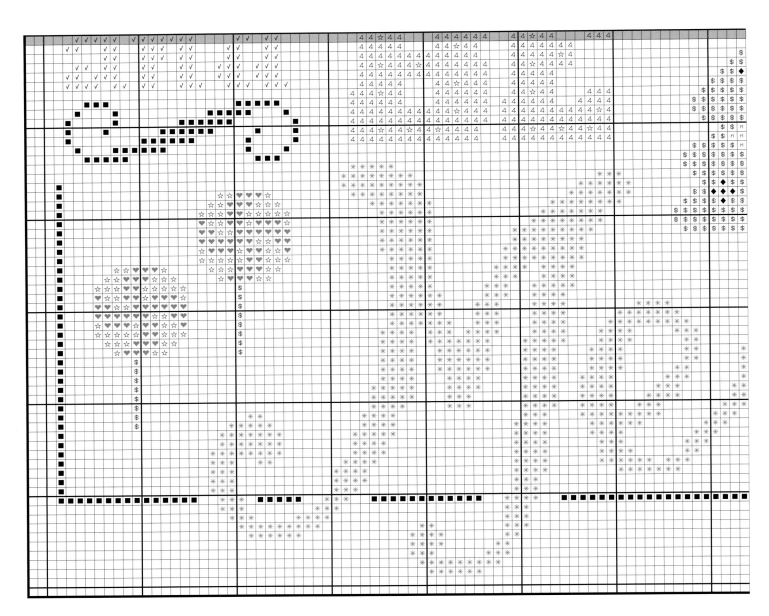

Eat Drink & Be Merry

X	DMC	COLOR
☆	blanc	white
⋒	209	lavender
♥	321	red
✎	407	sand
4	727	yellow
$	913	green

X	DMC	COLOR
7	948	peach
√	3340	apricot
◆	3689	mauve
✳	3766	teal
■	3799	vy dk grey
▨	Green areas indicate last rows of previous sections of design.	

Hello Old Friend

X	DMC	COLOR
☆	blanc	white (2 skeins)
✓	151	pink
■	310	black
♥	334	lt blue
▲	760	salmon

X	DMC	COLOR
◇	950	tan
▲	3072	grey
⊞	3828	brown
▨	Green areas indicate last rows of previous sections of design.	

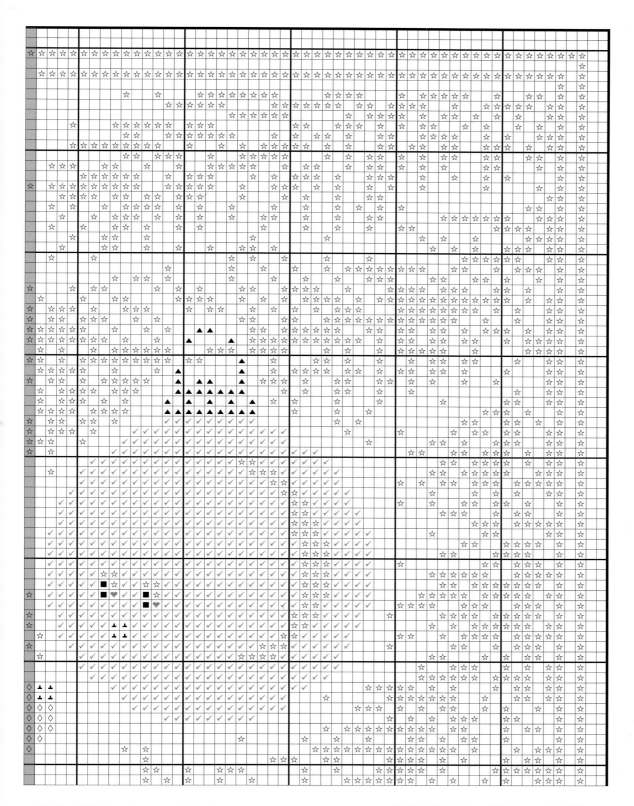

Hello Old Friend was stitched over two fabric threads on a 14$^1/_2$" x 14$^1/_2$" piece of 28 count Blue Glass Monaco Evenweave *(approx. design size: 8$^1/_2$" x 8$^1/_2$")* using two strands of embroidery floss for Cross Stitches. The design was framed in a 10" x 10" frame.

Hello Old Friend(118w x 118h)
14 count 8$^1/_2$" x 8$^1/_2$"
16 count 7$^3/_8$" x 7$^3/_8$"
18 count 6$^5/_8$" x 6$^5/_8$"

Hello Old Friend

X	DMC	COLOR
☆	blanc	white (2 skeins)
✓	151	pink
■	310	black
♥	334	lt blue
⊥	760	salmon
◇	950	tan
▲	3072	grey
⊞	3828	brown
▦	Green areas indicate last rows of previous sections of design.	

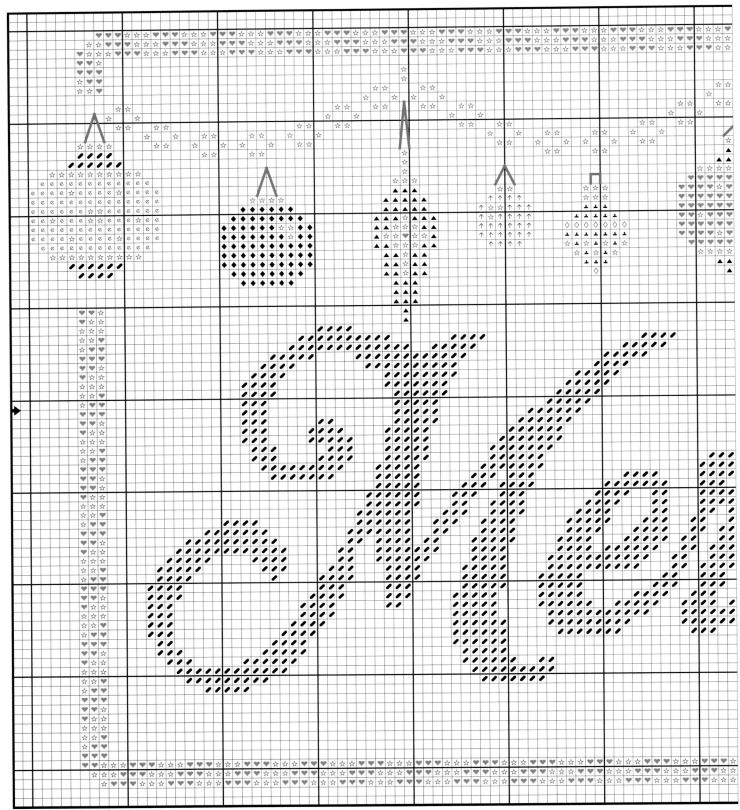

Merry Christmas

Merry Christmas (251w x 82h)

14 count 18" x 5⅞"
16 count 15¾" x 5⅛"
18 count 14" x 4⅝"

X	DMC	B'ST	COLOR		X	DMC	B'ST	COLOR
☆	blanc	∕	white		✓	564		lt jade
▲	151		pink		⊥	745		lt yellow
✖	210		lavender		◗	747		lt aqua (2 skeins)
◇	307		bright yellow		e	813		blue
◆	369		lt green		♥	3806		dk pink

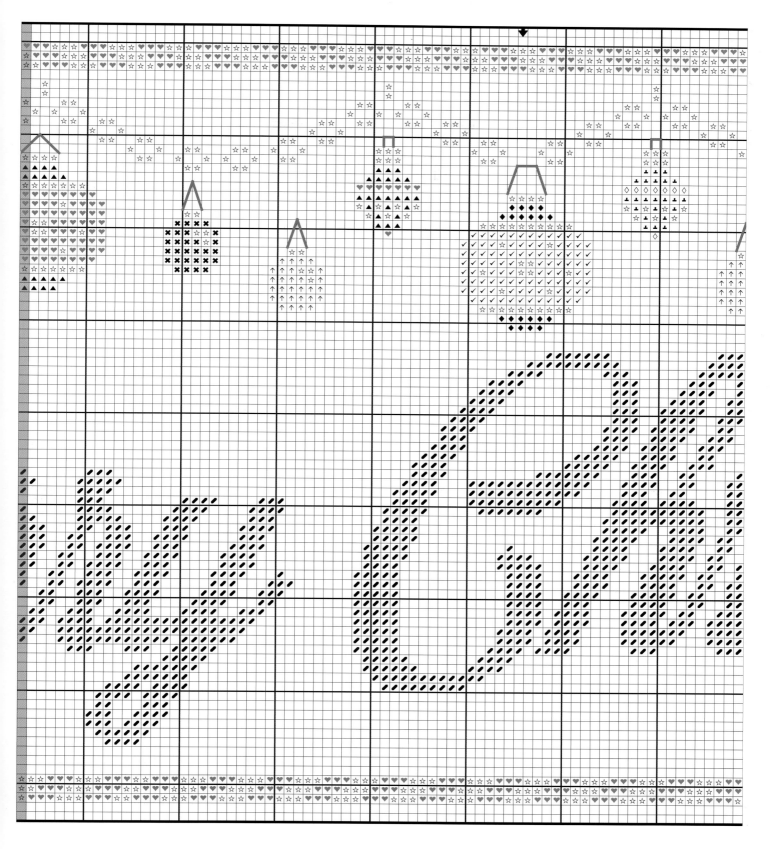

X	DMC	B'ST	COLOR
↑	3840		lt blue
▓	Green areas indicate last rows of previous sections of design.		

Merry Christmas was stitched over two fabric threads on a 24" x 12" piece of 28 count Tea Dyed Monaco Evenweave *(approx. design size: 18" x 5⁷/₈")* using two strands of embroidery floss for Cross Stitches and one strand of floss for Backstitches. The design was made into a basket band (see page 25).

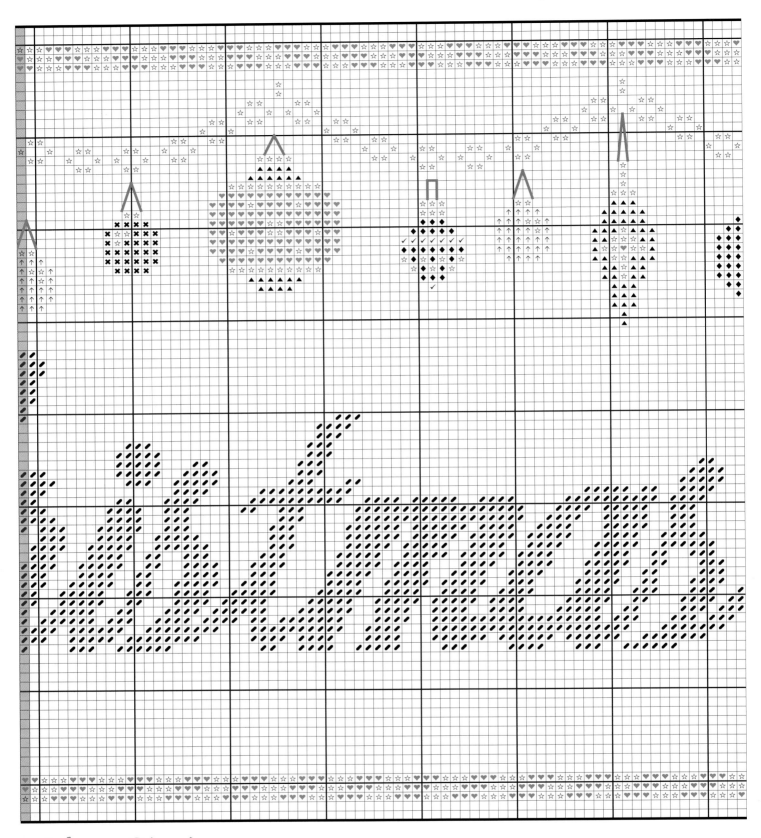

Merry Christmas

X	DMC	B'ST	COLOR		X	DMC	B'ST	COLOR
☆	blanc	╱	white		✓	564		lt jade
▲	151		pink		⊡	745		lt yellow
✖	210		lavender		✦	747		lt aqua (2 skeins)
◇	307		bright yellow		e	813		blue
◆	369		lt green		♥	3806		dk pink

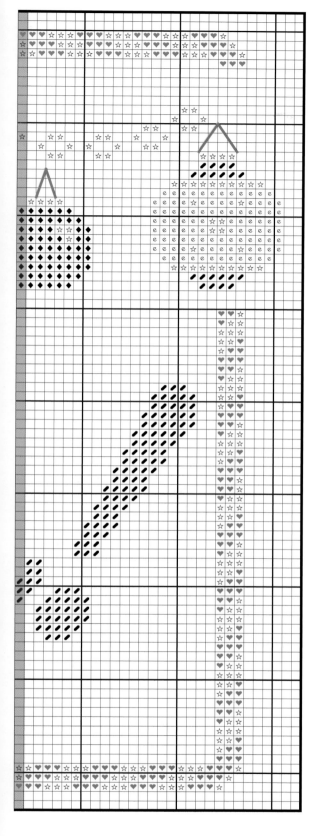

BASKET BAND

You'll need fabric for band (we used 2½ yards for our 20½" x 14½" x 9½" basket), hook and loop fastener tape, and lightweight fusible interfacing (we used 3 yards).

When sewing, always match the right sides and raw edges and use a ½" seam allowance.

1. Trim the stitched piece to the desired height plus ½" on the top and bottom. Trim the side edges so that they are even on both ends. Follow the manufacturer's instructions to fuse interfacing to the wrong side of the stitched piece.

2. Measure around the basket; add 6".

3. For the side fabric band pieces, divide the measurement determined in Step 2 in half and cut two fabric pieces the determined length by the same height as the trimmed stitched piece (from Step 1).

4. For the top and bottom fabric band pieces, measure the height of the basket for the area you wish to cover with the band. Subtract the height of the trimmed stitched piece. Add 1". Cut two fabric pieces the length determined in Step 2 by the determined height.

5. Fuse interfacing to the wrong side of all fabric pieces.

6. For the band front, sew the side band pieces to the stitched piece. Press the seam allowances open. Sew the top and bottom bands to the stitched piece and side bands. Press the seam allowances open.

7. For the band lining, cut a fabric piece the same size as the band front. Leaving one short end open, sew the front and lining pieces together. Clip the corners, turn right side out, and press.

8. Sew the hook side of the fastener tape to the wrong side of the finished end. Press the short raw edges ½" to the wrong side and slip stitch closed. Wrap the band around the basket and mark the position for the loop side of the fastener. Sew the fastener loop piece in place.

X	DMC	B'ST	COLOR
↑	3840		lt blue
▨	Green areas indicate last rows of previous sections of design.		

And To All A Good Night (108w x 116h)
14 count 7¾" x 8⅜"
16 count 6¾" x 7¼"
18 count 6" x 6½"

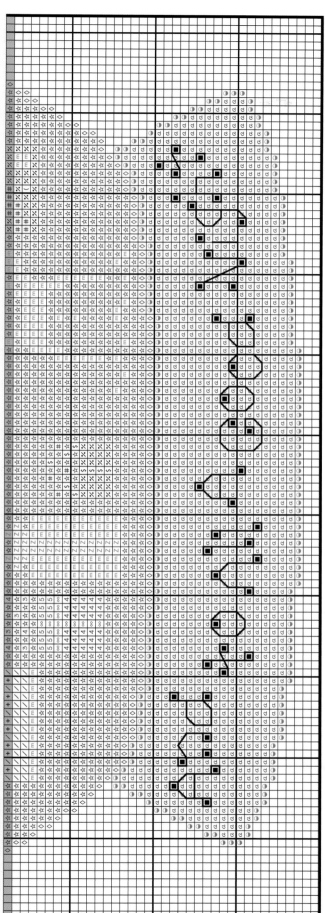

And To All A Good Night

And To All A Good Night was stitched over two fabric threads on a 14" x 14½" piece of 28 count Glass Blue Monaco Evenweave (*approx. design size: 7¾" x 8⅜"*) using two strands of embroidery floss for Cross Stitches and Quarter Stitches and one strand of floss for Backstitches and French Knots. The design was made into a hanging pillow (see page 28).

X	DMC	¼X	B'ST	COLOR
☆	blanc	H	*	white
#	151			rose
s	209			dk lavender
–	368			lt green
4	369			vy lt green
▶	453			grey
✦	666	◀	*	red
5	703			bright green
6	739			lt tan
◇	747	◇		lt aqua
a	841			dk beige
a	842			beige
✕	894			lt pink
3	907			avocado green

X	DMC	¼X	B'ST	COLOR
Z	956			coral
+	964			lt blue-green
7	977			lt hazel
◌	3078			pale yellow
⌐	3766			aqua
■	3799		Z	dk grey
✱	3810			turquoise
○	3843			bright blue
/	3844			dk turquoise
m	3846			lt turquoise
●	3799			French Knot
○	00479 Mill Hill Glass Seed Bead			
▨				Green area indicate last row of previous section of design.

*Work ¾ stitches.

And To All A Good Night

HANGING PILLOW

You'll need fabric for pillow back, silver cord for hanger lightweight fusible interfacing, and polyester fiberfill.

When sewing, always match the right sides and raw edges and use a 1/2" seam allowance.

1. For the pillow front, fuse interfacing to the wrong side of the stitched piece. Trim the stitched piece to the desired finished size and shape plus 1/2" on all sides. Cut a piece of fabric, in reverse, for the pillow back. Cut a 10" length of silver cord for the hanger; tie a knot close to each cord end.

2. Determine the cord hanger placement. Matching the cord ends to the fabric raw edges, baste the cord ends to the pillow front, leaving about 8" for the hanger.

3. Sew the pillow front and back together, leaving an opening for turning and being careful not to catch the hanger in the stitching. Clip the seam allowances as necessary, turn right side out, and press. Firmly stuff with fiberfill; slipstitch the opening closed.

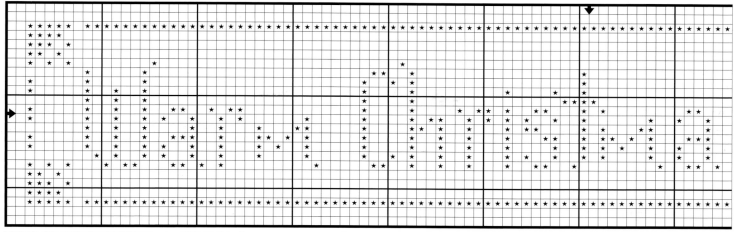

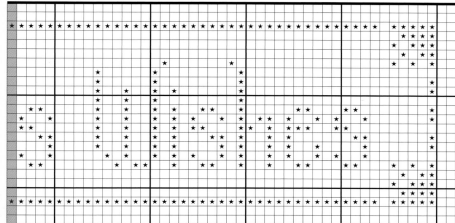

Warm Christmas Wishes

Warm Christmas Wishes (118w x 20h)
14 count 8^1/$_2$" x 1^1/$_2$"
16 count 7^3/$_8$" x 1^1/$_4$"
18 count 6^5/$_8$" x 1^1/$_8$"

X	DMC	COLOR
★	964	mint
▓	Green area indicates last row of previous section of design.	

Warm Christmas Wishes was stitched on 14 count Midnight Black Painted Perforated Paper *(approx. design size: 8^1/$_2$" x 1^1/$_2$")* using three strands of embroidery floss for Cross Stitches. The design was made into a shelf sitter.

SHELF SITTER

You'll need fabric, mat board or sturdy cardboard, black cardstock, double-sided tape, and craft glue.

1. Trim the stitched piece 4 stitches from the design on all sides. Use small pieces of double-sided tape to adhere the stitched piece to the black cardstock. Trim the cardstock to the same size as the stitched piece.

2. Cut a 10^1/$_2$" x 3^1/$_2$" mat board piece. Cut a 14^1/$_2$" x 7^1/$_2$"fabric piece. Cover the mat board with the fabric, wrapping the excess to the back and neatly gluing the fabric to the wrong side of the mat board. Allow to dry.

3. Adhere the stitched piece to the covered mat board with double-sided tape.

General Instructions

HOW TO READ CHARTS

Each design is made up of a key and a charted pattern on which each square represents a stitch. The symbols in the key indicate which floss color to use for each stitch on the chart. The following headings and symbols are given:

X – Cross Stitch

DMC – DMC color number

¹/₄ X – One-Quarter or Three-Quarter Stitch

B'ST – Backstitch

COLOR – the name given to the floss color in the chart

☐ A square filled with a full-size symbol should be stitched as a **Cross Stitch**.

☐ A reduced symbol in a corner of the square should be worked as a **One-Quarter Stitch** or a **Three-Quarter Stitch**.

☐ A straight line should be worked as a **Backstitch**.

☐ A large dot listed near the end of the key should be worked as a **French Knot**.

☐ An oval listed near the end of the key should be worked as a **Lazy Daisy Stitch**. The chart will indicate exact size and placement.

Sometimes the symbol for a **Cross Stitch** will be partially covered when a **Backstitch**, **French Knot**, or **Lazy Daisy Stitch** covers that square.

GETTING STARTED

How to Determine Finished Size

The finished size of your design will depend on the thread count per inch of the fabric being used. To determine the finished size of the design on different fabrics, divide the number of squares (stitches) in the width of the charted design by the thread count of the fabric. For example, a charted design with a width of 80 squares worked on 14 count Aida will yield a design 5³/₄" wide. Repeat for the number of squares (stitches) in the height of the charted design. Then add the amount of background you want plus a generous amount for finishing.

Preparing Fabric

Cut your fabric at least 3" larger on all sides than the design and overcast the edges to keep from fraying. It is better to waste a little fabric than to come up short.

Working with Floss

To ensure smoother stitches, separate floss into individual strands; then, realign them before threading the needle. Keep stitching tension consistent. Begin and end floss by running under several stitches on the back; never tie knots.

Where to Start

The horizontal and vertical centers of each charted design are shown by arrows. You may start at any point on the charted design, but be sure the design will be centered on the fabric. Locate the center of the fabric by folding it in half, top to bottom and again left to right. On the charted design, count the number of squares (stitches) from the center of the chart to where you wish to start. Then, from the fabric's center, find your starting point by counting out the same number of fabric threads (stitches).

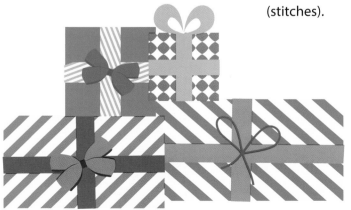

HOW TO STITCH

Always work **Cross Stitches** and **Quarter Stitches** first; then add the **Backstitch**, **French Knots**, and **Lazy Daisy Stitches**.

When stitching, bring the threaded needle up at 1 and all odd numbers and down at 2 and all even numbers.

Cross Stitch (X): Work stitches in two journeys *(Fig. 1)*. When working over two fabric threads, work Cross Stitches as shown in **Fig. 2**.

Fig. 1

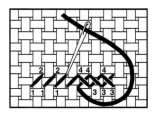

Fig. 2

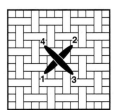

Quarter Stitch (¹/₄X): Stitch 1-2 is the **One-Quarter Stitch (¹/₄X)** *(Fig. 3)*. When stitches 1-4 are stitched in the same color, the resulting stitch is called a **Three-Quarter Stitch** and will be indicated on the color key. **Fig. 4** shows the technique for Quarter Stitches when working over two fabric threads.

Fig. 3

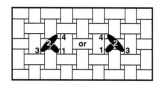

Fig. 4

Backstitch (B'ST): For outlines and details, Backstitch should be stitched after the design has been completed *(Fig. 5)*. When working over two fabric threads, work Backstitch as shown in **Fig. 6**.

Fig. 5

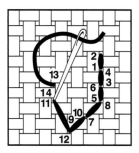

Fig. 6

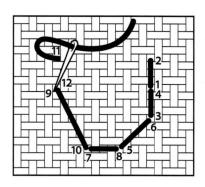

French Knot (Fr. Knot): Bring the needle up at 1. Wrap the floss once around the needle. Insert the needle at 2, tighten the knot, and pull the needle through the fabric, holding the floss until it must be released *(Fig. 7)*. For a larger knot, use more floss strands and wrap only once.

Fig. 7

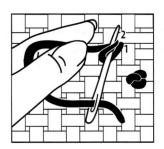

Attaching Beads

Use one strand of floss and a fine needle that will pass through the bead. Secure floss on the back of the fabric. Each bead is secured with a cross stitch so that it sits upright on the fabric. Bring the needle up at 1, run the needle through the bead and then down at 2. Bring needle up at 3, run the needle through the bead and then down at 4. Secure floss on the back or move to the next bead (*Fig. 8*).

Fig. 8

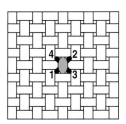

Meet the Designer: Lee Fisher

Lee Fisher of StitchyFish Designs considers needlework a classical art that uses colored threads to portray images from daily life — hopefully with a little whimsy and sense of humor.

"I would like to have my hand in creating designs which will interest a new generation of stitchers to carry on the tradition," she says. "I love the historical significance of working with the needle, the feeling of being connected in that way to the past."

Taught cross stitch at age 13 by her grandmother, Lee favors stitching scenes and sayings to frame, as well as pillows, ornaments, biscornus, and other accessories.

Lee designed her own projects for more than 20 years while working in the medical field and business. Now she designs full time.

She says she especially enjoyed creating the designs in this book. "Who doesn't love Christmas? When designing these, I loved traveling back in my mind to the Christmases of my childhood, remembering the images of the Atomic Era and the retro color palette of pinks, turquoise, burnt orange, and soft greens, which I am in love with."

Lee has three grown children, six grandchildren, two dogs, and a cat. She and her husband, Derek, enjoy collaborating on graphic novels, gardening, outdoor sports, and cultural events.

We have made every effort to ensure that these instructions are accurate and complete. We cannot, however, be responsible for human error, typographical mistakes, or variations in individual work.

Production Team: Technical Writer – Mary Sullivan Hutcheson; Technical Associates – Lisa Lancaster and Jean Lewis; Editorial Writer – Susan Frantz Wiles; Senior Graphic Artist – Lora Puls; Graphic Artist – Victoria Temple; Photostylist – Lori Wenger; Photographer – Jason Masters.

Cover items stitched by Kandi Ashford, Pam Essary, Joyce Harris, Gary Hutcheson, Phyllis Lundy, Donna Overman, and Anne Simpson.